GUIDED SCRIPTURE

THE GOSPEL OF MATTHEW

SECRET CHURCH

ISBN: 979-8-9855655-6-0

Copyright © 2025 by David Platt and Radical, Inc.

All rights reserved.

Printed in the United States of America.

Published by Radical, Inc.

Unless otherwise noted, all Scripture is from the ESV® Bible,
(The Holy Bible, English Standard Version), copyright© by Crossway.
Used by permission. All rights reserved.

WHY THE BOOK OF MATTHEW?

We're all hard-wired to want to make our lives count. None of us wants to get to the end of life, look back, and realize, "I missed the point." So how do we make our lives count? This step-by-step journey through the life of Jesus in the book of Matthew will reveal a clear answer to that question.

And for all who are bold enough to follow his lead, by God's grace we are guaranteed to get to the end of our time in this world and realize, **"My life counted for what matters most."**

TABLE OF CONTENTS

Introduction	03
About David Platt	16
About Radical	17
SESSION 01 Following Jesus and Making Him Known In Our Neighborhoods and All Nations	18
SESSION 02 Entrusting Our Lives and Spreading His Love	42
SESSION 03 Rest in the King as Agents of His Kingdom	72
SESSION 04 The Church: The Community of People Making Their Lives Count	96
Answer Key	132

Tonight Your Generosity Can Fuel Gospel Growth in Red Zones

RADICAL.NET/SCGIVE

Among the Unreached for the Unreached

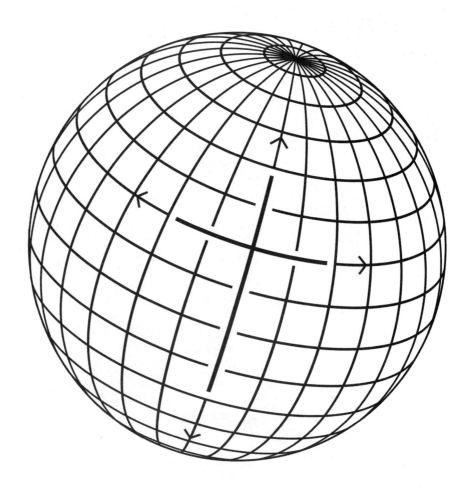

APPLY TODAY →
RADICAL.NET/TRAINING

Articles, Messages, Secret Church Archives, Videos & More

RADICAL.NET

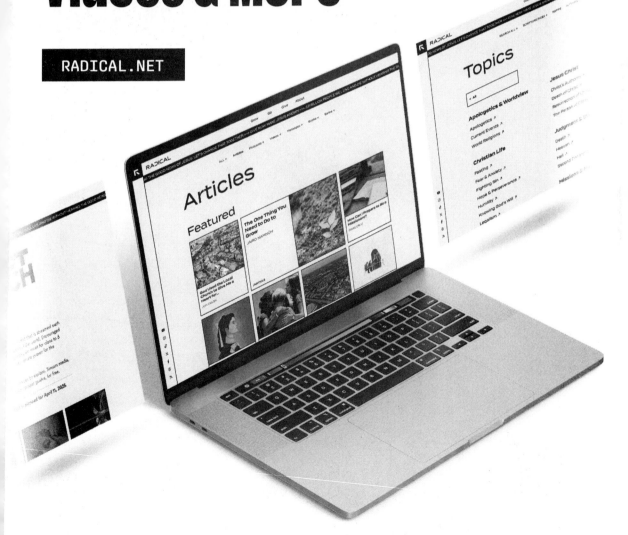

NEIGHBORHOODS

Apparel with Purpose

USE CODE **MATTHEW25** TO GET 25% OFF NOW THROUGH APRIL 30, 2025.

THE COMMISSION

RADICAL'S NEWSLETTER WITH
CURATED STORIES AND EXCLUSIVE CONTENT
TO HELP YOU MAKE YOUR LIFE COUNT FOREVER
BY FOLLOWING JESUS AND MAKING HIM KNOWN.

SIGN UP TODAY ↗
RADICAL.NET/COMMISSION

A Simple Guide to Deeper Intimacy with God

RECEIVE DAVID PLATT'S LATEST BOOK
FOR A GIFT OF ANY AMOUNT.

How To Read The Bible

A Simple Guide to Deeper Intimacy with God

David Platt

ABOUT
David Platt

David Platt serves as a Lead Pastor for McLean Bible Church. He is also the Founder and Chairman of Radical, an organization that helps people follow Jesus and make him known in their neighborhood and all nations. David received his B.A. from the University of Georgia and M.Div., Th.M., and Ph.D. from New Orleans Baptist Theological Seminary. Some of his published works include *Radical, Follow Me, Counter Culture, Something Needs to Change, Don't Hold Back, and How to Read the Bible.* He lives in the Washington, D.C. metro area with his wife and children.

ABOUT
Radical

Radical helps people around the world follow Jesus and make him known in their neighborhoods and all nations. We exist to help people make their lives count for what matters most.

To do this, we...

- Engage millions of people globally with gospel content through a variety of creative mediums.
- Enable thousands of gospel leaders with resources to work among the least reached people on the planet.

FOLLOWING JESUS AND MAKING HIM KNOWN IN OUR NEIGHBORHOODS AND ALL NATIONS

Do you want your life to count?

How do you make your life count?

spreading the word of God and serving others

THE BOOK OF MATTHEW IS A _gospel_

(AN ACCOUNT OF GOOD NEWS!).

It is not a congregational letter.

It is not a comprehensive biography.

It is not a chronological history.

MATTHEW 7:28-29

28 And when Jesus (finished) these sayings, the crowds were astonished at his teaching, 29 for he was teaching them as one who had authority, and not as their scribes.

MATTHEW 11:1

¹ When Jesus had (finished) ② instructing his twelve disciples, he went on from there to teach and preach in their cities.

MATTHEW 13:53

⁵³ And when Jesus had (finished) ③ these parables, he went away from there,

MATTHEW 19:1

¹ Now when Jesus had (finished) ④ these sayings, he went away from Galilee and entered the region of Judea beyond the Jordan.

MATTHEW 26:1-2

¹ When Jesus had (finished) ⑤ all these sayings, he said to his disciples, ² "You know that after two days the Passover is coming, and the Son of Man will be delivered up to be crucified."

Accounts of Jesus' words + works

BOOK OF MATTHEW | SESSION 01

THE BOOK OF MATTHEW IS ONE OF __Four__ GOSPELS.

MATTHEW 1:1-16

¹ The book of the genealogy of Jesus Christ, the son of David, the son of Abraham. ² Abraham was the father of Isaac, and Isaac the father of Jacob, and Jacob the father of Judah and his brothers, ³ and Judah the father of Perez and Zerah by Tamar, and Perez the father of Hezron, and Hezron the father of Ram, ⁴ and Ram the father of Amminadab, and Amminadab the father of Nahshon, and Nahshon the father of Salmon, ⁵ and Salmon the father of Boaz by Rahab, and Boaz the father of Obed by Ruth, and Obed the father of Jesse, ⁶ and Jesse the father of David the king.

And David was the father of Solomon by the wife of Uriah, ⁷ and Solomon the father of Rehoboam, and Rehoboam the father of Abijah, and Abijah the father of Asaph, ⁸ and Asaph the father of Jehoshaphat, and

14 generations to David

Jehoshaphat the father of Joram, and Joram the father of Uzziah, ⁹ and Uzziah the father of Jotham, and Jotham the father of Ahaz, and Ahaz the father of Hezekiah, ¹⁰ and Hezekiah the father of Manasseh, and Manasseh the father of Amos, and Amos the father of Josiah, ¹¹ and Josiah the father of Jechoniah and his brothers, at the time of the deportation to Babylon.

¹² And after the deportation to Babylon: Jechoniah was the father of Shealtiel, and Shealtiel the father of Zerubbabel, ¹³ and Zerubbabel the father of Abiud, and Abiud the father of Eliakim, and Eliakim the father of Azor, ¹⁴ and Azor the father of Zadok, and Zadok the father of Achim, and Achim the father of Eliud, ¹⁵ and Eliud the father of Eleazar, and Eleazar the father of Matthan, and Matthan the father of Jacob, ¹⁶ and Jacob the father of Joseph the husband of Mary, of whom Jesus was born, who is called Christ.

BOOK OF MATTHEW | SESSION 01

MATTHEW 1:1

¹ The book of the genealogy of Jesus Christ, the son of David, the son of Abraham.

TWENTY PICTURES OF JESUS

1. JESUS IS THE **Savior**.

Joshua → Yahweh

MATTHEW 1:21

²¹ She will bear a son, and you shall call his name Jesus, for he will save his people from their sins."

2. JESUS IS THE **Messiah**.

3. JESUS IS THE SON OF DAVID.

MATTHEW 1:17

¹⁷ So all the generations from Abraham to David were fourteen generations, and from

David to the deportation to Babylon **fourteen** generations, and from the deportation to Babylon to the Christ **fourteen** generations.

[handwritten: 14 - DAVID]

(See 2 Sam. 7:1-29; Isa. 9:6-7; 11:1-10; Jer. 23:5-6; Ezek. 37:24-25)

4. JESUS IS THE SON OF ABRAHAM.

GENESIS 12:1-3

¹ Now the Lord said to Abram, "Go from your country and your kindred and your father's house to the land that I will show you. ² And I will make of you a great nation, and I will bless you and make your name great, so that you will be a blessing. ³ I will bless those who bless you, and him who dishonors you I will curse, and in you all the families of the earth shall be blessed."

[handwritten margin note: A covenant people]

God will form a covenant people.

God will give them a promised inheritance on Earth.

God will use them to accomplish a global purpose.

GENESIS 17:6

⁶ I will make you exceedingly fruitful, and I will make you into nations, and kings shall come from you.

He will send a King.

GENESIS 17:15-16

¹⁵ And God said to Abraham, "As for Sarai your wife, you shall not call her name Sarai, but Sarah shall be her name. ¹⁶ I will bless her, and moreover, I will give you a son by her.

I will bless her, and she shall become nations;

kings of peoples shall come from her."

His kingdom will one day expand to all people groups.

GENESIS 49:10

¹⁰ The scepter shall not depart from Judah,

nor the ruler's staff from between his feet,

until tribute comes to him;

and to him shall be the obedience of the

peoples.

5. JESUS IS THE ___center___ OF ALL HISTORY.

MATTHEW 1:18

¹⁸ Now the birth of Jesus Christ took place in this way. When his mother Mary had been betrothed to Joseph, before they came together she was found to be with child from the Holy Spirit.

MATTHEW 1:19-20

19 And her husband Joseph, being a just man and unwilling to put her to shame, resolved to divorce her quietly. 20 But as he considered these things, behold, an angel of the Lord appeared to him in a dream, saying, "Joseph, son of David, do not fear to take Mary as your wife, for that which is conceived in her is from the Holy Spirit.

MATTHEW 1:21-25

Jesus means Yahweh

21 She will bear a son, and you shall call his name Jesus, for he will save his people from their sins." 22 All this took place to fulfill what the Lord had spoken by the prophet:

23 "Behold, the virgin shall conceive and bear a son,
   and they shall call his name Immanuel"

> (which means, God with us). ²⁴ When Joseph woke from sleep, he did as the angel of the Lord commanded him: he took his wife, ²⁵ but knew her not until she had given birth to a son. And he called his name Jesus.

6. JESUS IS FULLY ___Human___.

7. JESUS IS FULLY ___Divine___.

MATHHEW 1:16

> ¹⁶ and Jacob the father of Joseph the husband of Mary, of whom Jesus was born, who is called Christ.

Joseph never referr to as Jesus' Father
Incarnation

> God is the Creator and Re-Creator of all things.

Genesis = the origin of Messiah

MATTHEW 1:18a

¹⁸ Now the <u>birth</u> of Jesus Christ took place in this way.

GENESIS 1:1-2

¹ In the <u>beginning</u>, God created the heavens and the earth. ² The earth was without form and void, and darkness was over the face of the deep. And the Spirit of God was hovering over the face of the waters.

In Genesis, the Spirit brings life to men.

In Matthew, the Spirit gives life to the Messiah.

GENESIS 3:15

¹⁵ I will put enmity between you and the woman, and between your offspring and her offspring;

>   he shall bruise your head,
>   and you shall bruise his heel."

In Genesis, God promises a seed from a woman.

In Matthew, God delivers that seed through a woman.

ROMANS 5:12-14

¹² Therefore, just as sin came into the world through one man, and death through sin, and so death spread to all men because all sinned— ¹³ for sin indeed was in the world before the law was given, but sin is not counted where there is no law. ¹⁴ Yet death reigned from Adam to Moses, even over those whose sinning was not like the transgression of Adam, who was a type of the one who was to come.

> In Genesis, a <u>man is born</u> who would <u>succumb to sin.</u>

> In Matthew, a <u>man is born</u> who would <u>save from sin.</u>

> God is both transcendent over us and ___present___ with us.

Immanuel: God with us →

8. JESUS IS THE SOVEREIGN OVER THE WISE (MATT. 2:1-12).

9. JESUS IS THE SHEPHERD OF THE ___weak___ (MATT. 2:6; MIC. 5:2).

10. JESUS INAUGURATES A NEW EXODUS (MATT. 2:13-15).

11. JESUS ENDS THE MOURNFUL EXILE (MATT. 2:16-18).

12. JESUS LOVES HIS FIERCEST __enemies__ (MATT. 2:19-23).

13. JESUS IS THE SAVIOR KING (MATT. 3:1-3).

14. JESUS IS THE RIGHTEOUS __judge__ (MATT. 3:12).

15. JESUS IS FILLED WITH GOD THE SPIRIT.

> **MATTHEW 3:16-17**
>
> ¹⁶ And when Jesus was baptized, immediately he went up from the water, and behold, the heavens were opened to him, and he saw the Spirit of God descending like a dove and coming to rest on him; ¹⁷ and behold, a voice from heaven said, "This is <u>my beloved Son, with whom I am well pleased</u>."

16. JESUS IS LOVED BY GOD THE FATHER.

17. JESUS IS THE NEW ADAM (MATT. 4:1-11).

18. JESUS IS THE TRUE ~~Adam~~ Israel.

19. JESUS IS THE LIGHT OF THE WORLD.

MATTHEW 4:15-16

¹⁵ "The land of Zebulun and the land of Naphtali,

the way of the sea, beyond the Jordan,

Galilee of the Gentiles—

¹⁶ the people dwelling in darkness

have seen a great light,

and for those dwelling in the region and

shadow of death,

on them a light has dawned."

20. JESUS IS THE HOPE FOR ALL Nations.

MATTHEW 4:18-22

¹⁸ While walking by the Sea of Galilee, he saw two brothers, Simon (who is called Peter)

and Andrew his brother, casting a net into the sea, for they were fishermen. ¹⁹ And he said to them, "Follow me, and I will make you fishers of men." ²⁰ Immediately they left their nets and followed him. ²¹ And going on from there he saw two other brothers, James the son of Zebedee and John his brother, in the boat with Zebedee their father, mending their nets, and he called them. ²² Immediately they left the boat and their father and followed him.

Jesus is worthy of far more than casual association.

Jesus is worthy of supreme __Adoration__.

THE LIFE THAT COUNTS __follows__ JESUS.

Life is found in dying to __sin__.

MATTHEW 4:17

¹⁷ From that time Jesus began to preach, saying, "Repent, for the kingdom of heaven is at hand."

Life is found in dying to ___self___.

- Comfort
- Careers
- Possessions } Renounce
- Position
- Families
- Friends
- Safety

MATTHEW 13:44

⁴⁴ "The kingdom of heaven is like <u>treasure</u> hidden in a <u>field</u>, which a man <u>found</u> and covered up. Then in his joy he goes and <u>sells</u> all that he has and <u>buys</u> that <u>field</u>.

He takes the initiative to __choose__ us.

This is not a call to a set of rules and regulations; this is a call to a __relationship__.

MATTHEW 4:19

¹⁹ And he said to them, "Follow me, and I will make you fishers of men."

THE LIFE THAT COUNTS __follows__ JESUS AND MAKES HIM __known__.

In your __neighborhood__.

In all __nations__.

MATTHEW 4:23-25

²³ And he went throughout all Galilee, teaching in their synagogues and proclaiming the gospel of the kingdom and healing every disease and every affliction among the people. ²⁴ So his fame spread throughout all Syria, and they brought him all the sick, those afflicted with various diseases and pains, those oppressed by demons, those having seizures, and paralytics, and he healed them. ²⁵ And great crowds followed him from Galilee and the Decapolis, and from Jerusalem and Judea, and from beyond the Jordan.

PRAYER MOMENT

PRAY THAT THE WORD OF THE LORD MAY SPEED AHEAD AND BE HONORED (2 THESSALONIANS 3:1)

- Pray for **followers of Jesus** all over the world who are faithfully and boldly proclaiming the gospel in their neighborhood and all nations.
  - Pray that they would clearly and compassionately share the truth, and that they would rely on the Holy Spirit to draw people to himself.
  - Pray that they would not be discouraged in this work and that they would continue to grow in this discipline.
- Pray for **local pastors** in places where healthy Christian churches are few and far between. Pray that they would lead their churches in humility and faithfulness to God and his Word.
- Pray that **more leaders** would be raised up within these churches, and for all the members of their congregation to make their life count by following Jesus and making him known.

GIVE TODAY ♥
MAKE JESUS KNOWN IN INDONESIA, NORTH KOREA, MYANMAR, AND OTHER HARD TO REACH PLACES.

RADICAL.NET/SCGIVE

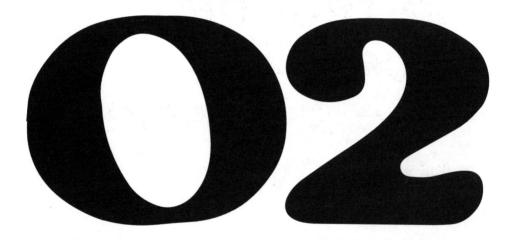

ENTRUSTING OUR LIVES AND SPREADING HIS LOVE

SUMMARY

THE LIFE THAT COUNTS FOLLOWS JESUS AND MAKES HIM KNOWN IN YOUR NEIGHBORHOOD AND ALL NATIONS (MATT. 1-4).

FOLLOWING JESUS MEANS ENTRUSTING OUR LIVES TO HIS AUTHORITY (MATT. 5-9).

MAKING JESUS KNOWN MEANS SPREADING HIS LOVE WITH HIS AUTHORITY (MATT. 10).

THE AUTHORITY OF JESUS' WORDS

MATTHEW 5:1-2

¹ Seeing the crowds, he went up on the mountain, and when he sat down, his disciples came to him. ² And he opened his mouth and taught them, saying:

MATTHEW 4:23

²³ And he went throughout all Galilee, teaching in their synagogues and proclaiming <u>the gospel of the kingdom</u>, of God and healing every disease and every affliction among the people.

TRUE (AND BETTER) HAPPINESS (MATT. 5:3-12)

MATTHEW 5:3

³ "<u>Blessed</u> are the <u>poor in spirit</u>, for theirs is the <u>kingdom of heaven</u>.

TRUE (AND BETTER) INFLUENCE (MATT. 5:13-16)

MATTHEW 5:16

¹⁶ In the same way, let your <u>light</u> shine before others, so that they may <u>see your good works</u> and <u>give</u> glory to your <u>Father</u> who is in heave<u>n</u>.

TRUE (AND BETTER) RIGHTEOUSNESS (MATT. 5:17-48)

MATTHEW 5:17

¹⁷ "Do not think that I have come to abolish the Law or the Prophets; I have not come to abolish them but to fulfill them.

MATTHEW 5:20

²⁰ For I tell you, unless your righteousness exceeds that of the scribes and Pharisees, you will never enter the kingdom of heaven.

Turning from Anger (Matt. 5:21-26)

Turning from Lust (Matt. 5:27-30)

Faithfulness in Marriage (Matt. 5:31-32)

Integrity in Speech (Matt. 5:33-37)

Not Retaliating When Wronged (Matt. 5:38-42)

Loving Your Enemy (Matt. 5:43-47)

MATTHEW 5:48

⁴⁸ You therefore must be perfect, as your heavenly Father is perfect.

TRUE (AND BETTER) RELIGION (MATT. 6:1-18)

Giving (Matt. 6:1-4)

Praying (Matt. 6:5-14)

Fasting (Matt. 6:16-18)

And your Father who sees in secret will reward you. (See Matthew 6:4b, 6b, 18b)

TRUE (AND BETTER) TREASURE (MATT. 6:19-24)

MATTHEW 6:19-20

¹⁹ "Do not lay up for yourselves treasures on earth, where moth and rust destroy and where thieves break in and steal, ²⁰ but lay up for yourselves treasures in heaven, where neither moth nor rust destroys and where thieves do not break in and steal.

TRUE (AND BETTER) TRUST (MATT. 6:25-34)

MATTHEW 6:33

³³ But seek first the kingdom of God and his righteousness, and all these things will be added to you.

TRUE (AND BETTER) RELATIONSHIPS

(MATT. 7:1-12)

MATTHEW 7:12

¹² "So whatever you wish that others would do to you, do also to them, for this is the Law and the Prophets.

TRUE (AND BETTER) DISCIPLESHIP

(MATT. 7:13-27)

> The Wide Gate/Easy Way and the Narrow Gate/Hard Way (Matt. 7:13-14)

> Bad Fruit and Good Fruit (Matt. 7:15-23)

> The Foolish Builder and the Wise Builder (Matt. 7:24-27)

MATTHEW 7:24

²⁴ "Everyone then who hears these words of mine and does them will be like a wise man who built his house on the rock.

MATTHEW 7:28-29

²⁸ And when Jesus finished these sayings, the crowds were astonished at his teaching, ²⁹ for he was teaching them as one who had authority, and not as their scribes.

THE LIFE THAT COUNTS SUBMITS TO THE AUTHORITY OF JESUS' __words__.

THE AUTHORITY OF JESUS' WORKS

Three Miracle Stories (Matt. 8:1-17)

Two Descriptions of Discipleship (Matt. 8:18-22)

BOOK OF MATTHEW | SESSION 02

Three Miracle Stories (Matt. 8:23-9:8)

Two Descriptions of Discipleship (Matt. 9:9-17)

Three Miracle Stories (Matt. 9:18-34)

JESUS HAS AUTHORITY OVER _Disease_.

MATTHEW 8:2-4

² And behold, a leper came to him and knelt before him, saying, "Lord, if you will, you can make me clean." ³ And Jesus stretched out his hand and touched him, saying, "I will; be clean." And immediately his leprosy was cleansed. ⁴ And Jesus said to him, "See that you say nothing to anyone, but go, show yourself to the priest and offer the gift that Moses commanded, for a proof to them."

He cleanses the physically unclean.

> He heals the ethnically outcast.

MATTHEW 8:6-13

⁶ "Lord, my servant is lying paralyzed at home, suffering terribly." ⁷ And he said to him, "I will come and heal him." ⁸ But the centurion replied, "Lord, I am not worthy to have you come under my roof, but only say the word, and my servant will be healed. ⁹ For I too am a man under authority, with soldiers under me. And I say to one, 'Go,' and he goes, and to another, 'Come,' and he comes, and to my servant, 'Do this,' and he does it." ¹⁰ When Jesus heard this, he marveled and said to those who followed him, "Truly, I tell you, with no one in Israel have I found such faith. ¹¹ I tell you, many will come from east and west and recline at table with Abraham, Isaac, and Jacob in the kingdom of heaven, ¹² while the sons of the kingdom will be thrown into the outer darkness. In that place there will be

weeping and gnashing of teeth." ¹³ And to the centurion Jesus said, "Go; let it be done for you as you have believed." And the servant was healed at that very moment.

He restores the culturally marginalized.

MATTHEW 8:14-17

¹⁴ And when Jesus entered Peter's house, he saw his mother-in-law lying sick with a fever. ¹⁵ He touched her hand, and the fever left her, and she rose and began to serve him. ¹⁶ That evening they brought to him many who were oppressed by demons, and he cast out the spirits with a word and healed all who were sick. ¹⁷ This was to fulfill what was spoken by the <u>prophet Isaiah</u>: "<u>He took our illnesses and bore our diseases</u>."

ISAIAH 53:5-6

⁵ But he was pierced for our transgressions;

  he was crushed for our iniquities;

 upon him was the chastisement that brought

   us peace,

 and with his wounds we are healed.

⁶ All we like sheep have gone astray;

  we have turned—every one—to his own

    way;

 and the Lord has laid on him

   the iniquity of us all.

JESUS HAS AUTHORITY OVER ~~all suffering~~ *disciples* (MATT. 8:18-22).

JESUS HAS AUTHORITY OVER ~~sin~~ *disaster*.

MATTHEW 8:23-27

²³ And when he got into the boat, his disciples followed him. ²⁴ And behold, there arose a great storm on the sea, so that the boat

was being swamped by the waves; but he was asleep. ²⁵ And they went and woke him, saying, "Save us, Lord; we are perishing." ²⁶ And he said to them, "Why are you afraid, O you of little faith?" Then he rose and rebuked the winds and the sea, and there was a great calm. ²⁷ And the men marveled, saying, "What sort of man is this, that even winds and sea obey him?"

YAHWEH

JESUS HAS AUTHORITY OVER ~~disaster~~ *demons*.

MATTHEW 8:28-32

²⁸ And when he came to the other side, to the country of the Gadarenes, two demon-possessed men met him, coming out of the tombs, so fierce that no one could pass that way. ²⁹ And behold, they cried out, "What have you to do with us, O Son of God? Have you come here to torment us before the time?"

Demons fear because of their belief
Men fear b/c lack of faith

⁣³⁰ Now a herd of many pigs was feeding at some distance from them. ³¹ And the demons begged him, saying, "If you cast us out, send us away into the herd of pigs." ³² And he said to them, "Go." So they came out and went into the pigs, and behold, the whole herd rushed down the steep bank into the sea and drowned in the waters.

JESUS HAS AUTHORITY OVER ~~Demons~~ **Sin**.

MATTHEW 9:1-8

¹ And getting into a boat he crossed over and came to his own city. ² And behold, some people brought to him a paralytic, lying on a bed. And when Jesus saw their faith, he said to the paralytic, "Take heart, my son; your sins are forgiven." ³ And behold, some of the scribes said to themselves, "This man is blaspheming." ⁴ But Jesus, knowing their

thoughts, said, "Why do you think evil in your hearts? ⁵ For which is easier, to say, 'Your sins are forgiven,' or to say, 'Rise and walk'? ⁶ But that you may know that the Son of Man has authority on earth to forgive sins"—he then said to the paralytic—"Rise, pick up your bed and go home." ⁷ And he rose and went home. ⁸ When the crowds saw it, they were afraid, and they glorified God, who had given such authority to men.

JESUS HAS AUTHORITY TO _forgive sins / save_.

MATTHEW 9:9-10

⁹ As Jesus passed on from there, he saw a man called Matthew sitting at the tax booth, and he said to him, "Follow me." And he rose and followed him. ¹⁰ And as Jesus reclined at table in the house, behold, many tax collectors and sinners came and were reclining with Jesus and his disciples.

JESUS HAS AUTHORITY OVER ___Death___.

MATTHEW 9:23-26

²³ And when Jesus came to the ruler's house and saw the flute players and the crowd making a commotion, ²⁴ he said, "Go away, for the girl is not dead but sleeping." And they laughed at him. ²⁵ But when the crowd had been put outside, he went in and took her by the hand, and the girl arose. ²⁶ And the report of this went through all that district.

JESUS HAS AUTHORITY OVER ___disability___.

MATTHEW 9:27-31

²⁷ And as Jesus passed on from there, two blind men followed him, crying aloud, "Have mercy on us, Son of David." ²⁸ When he entered the house, the blind men came to him, and Jesus said to them, "Do you believe that

I am able to do this?" They said to him, "Yes, Lord." ²⁹ Then he touched their eyes, saying, "According to your faith be it done to you." ³⁰ And their eyes were opened. And Jesus sternly warned them, "See that no one knows about it." ³¹ But they went away and spread his fame through all that district.

JESUS HAS AUTHORITY OVER THE __Devil__.

MATTHEW 9:32-34

³² As they were going away, behold, a demon-oppressed man who was mute was brought to him. ³³ And when the demon had been cast out, the mute man spoke. And the crowds marveled, saying, "Never was anything like this seen in Israel." ³⁴ But the Pharisees said, "He casts out demons by the prince of demons."

THE LIFE THAT COUNTS SUBMITS TO THE AUTHORITY OF JESUS' __work__.

FOLLOWING JESUS MEANS __entrusting__ OUR LIVES TO HIS AUTHORITY (MATT. 5-9).

MATTHEW 9:35-38

³⁵ And Jesus went throughout all the cities and villages, teaching in their synagogues and proclaiming the gospel of the kingdom and healing every disease and every affliction. ³⁶ When he saw the crowds, he had compassion for them, because they were harassed and helpless, like sheep without a shepherd. ³⁷ Then he said to his disciples, "The harvest is plentiful, but the laborers are few; ³⁸ therefore pray earnestly to the Lord of the harvest to send out laborers into his harvest."

ISAIAH 17:11b

yet the harvest will flee away

in a day of grief and incurable pain.

REVELATION 14:14-19

14 Then I looked, and behold, a white cloud, and seated on the cloud one like a son of man, with a golden crown on his head, and a sharp sickle in his hand. 15 And another angel came out of the temple, calling with a loud voice to him who sat on the cloud, "Put in your sickle, and reap, for the hour to reap has come, for the harvest of the earth is fully ripe." 16 So he who sat on the cloud swung his sickle across the earth, and the earth was reaped.
17 Then another angel came out of the temple in heaven, and he too had a sharp sickle.
18 And another angel came out from the altar, the angel who has authority over the fire, and he called with a loud voice to the one who had the sharp sickle, "Put in your sickle and gather the clusters from the vine of the earth, for its

grapes are ripe." ¹⁹ So the angel swung his sickle across the earth and gathered the grape harvest of the earth and threw it into the great winepress of the wrath of God.

MATTHEW 10:1

¹ And he called to him his twelve disciples and gave them authority over unclean spirits, to cast them out, and to heal every disease and every affliction.

MAKING JESUS KNOWN MEANS _spreading_ HIS LOVE WITH HIS AUTHORITY (MATT. 10).

MATTHEW 10:5-7

⁵ These twelve Jesus sent out, instructing them, "Go nowhere among the Gentiles and enter no town of the Samaritans, ⁶ but go rather to the lost sheep of the house of Israel. ⁷ And proclaim as you go, saying, 'The kingdom of heaven is at hand.'

Go to great __Need__.

MATTHEW 10:8-10

⁸ Heal the sick, raise the dead, cleanse lepers, cast out demons. You received without paying; give without pay. ⁹ Acquire no gold or silver or copper for your belts, ¹⁰ no bag for your journey, or two tunics or sandals or a staff, for the laborer deserves his food.

Go to great __danger__.

MATTHEW 10:11-16

¹¹ And whatever town or village you enter, find out who is worthy in it and stay there until you depart. ¹² As you enter the house, greet it. ¹³ And if the house is worthy, let your peace come upon it, but if it is not worthy, let your peace return to you. ¹⁴ And if anyone will not

receive you or listen to your words, shake off the dust from your feet when you leave that house or town. ¹⁵ Truly, I say to you, it will be more bearable on the day of judgment for the land of Sodom and Gomorrah than for that town. ¹⁶ "Behold, I am sending you out as sheep in the midst of wolves, so be wise as serpents and innocent as doves.

MATTHEW 10:17-20

¹⁷ Beware of men, for they will deliver you over to courts and flog you in their synagogues, ¹⁸ and you will be dragged before governors and kings for my sake, to bear witness before them and the Gentiles. ¹⁹ When they deliver you over, do not be anxious how you are to speak or what you are to say, for what you are to say will be given to you in that hour. ²⁰ For it is not you who speak, but the Spirit of your Father speaking through you.

You will be ___betrayed___.

MATTHEW 10:21

²¹ Brother will deliver brother over to death, and the father his child, and children will rise against parents and have them put to death,

You will be hated.

MATTHEW 10:22

²² and you will be hated by all for my name's sake. But the one who endures to the end will be saved.

You will be persecuted.

BOOK OF MATTHEW | SESSION 02

MATTHEW 10:23

²³ When they persecute you in one town, flee to the next, for truly, I say to you, you will not have gone through all the towns of Israel before the Son of Man comes.

MATTHEW 10:24-25

²⁴ "A disciple is not above his teacher, nor a servant above his master. ²⁵ It is enough for the disciple to be like his teacher, and the servant like his master. If they have called the master of the house Beelzebul, how much more will they malign those of his household.

_____Fear_____ will tempt you.

MATTHEW 10:26-31

²⁶ "So have no fear of them, for nothing is covered that will not be revealed, or hidden

that will not be known. ²⁷ What I tell you in the dark, say in the light, and what you hear whispered, proclaim on the housetops. ²⁸ And do not fear those who kill the body but cannot kill the soul. Rather fear him who can destroy both soul and body in hell. ²⁹ Are not two sparrows sold for a penny? And not one of them will fall to the ground apart from your Father. ³⁰ But even the hairs of your head are all numbered. ³¹ Fear not, therefore; you are of more value than many sparrows.

Do Not Fear!!

The **Father** will take care of you.

Acknowledge him **publicly**.

MATTHEW 10:32-33

³² So everyone who acknowledges me before men, I also will acknowledge before my Father

BOOK OF MATTHEW | SESSION 02

who is in heaven, ³³ but whoever denies me before men, I also will deny before my Father who is in heaven.

Love him ~~supremly~~ **supremely**

MATTHEW 10:34-37

³⁴ "Do not think that I have come to bring peace to the earth. I have not come to bring peace, but a sword. ³⁵ For I have come to set a man against his father, and a daughter against her mother, and a daughter-in-law against her mother-in-law. ³⁶ And a person's enemies will be those of his own household. ³⁷ Whoever loves father or mother more than me is not worthy of me, and whoever loves son or daughter more than me is not worthy of me.

Take the ultimate **risk**.

MATTHEW 10:38-39

⁳⁸ And whoever does not take his cross and follow me is not worthy of me. ³⁹ Whoever finds his life will lose it, and whoever loses his life for my sake will find it.

Find the ultimate __reward__.

MATTHEW 10:40-42

⁴⁰ "Whoever receives you receives me, and whoever receives me receives him who sent me. ⁴¹ The one who receives a prophet because he is a prophet will receive a prophet's reward, and the one who receives a righteous person because he is a righteous person will receive a righteous person's reward. ⁴² And whoever gives one of these little ones even a cup of cold water because he is a disciple, truly, I say to you, he will by no means lose his reward.

FOLLOWING JESUS MEANS ENTRUSTING OUR LIVES TO HIS AUTHORITY (MATT. 5-9).

MAKING JESUS KNOWN MEANS SPREADING HIS LOVE WITH HIS AUTHORITY (MATT. 10).

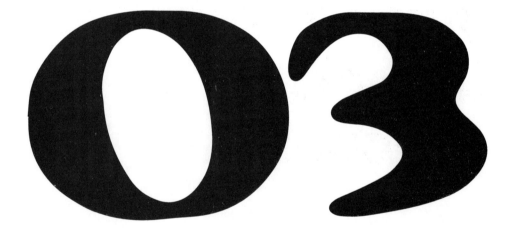

REST IN THE KING AS AGENTS OF HIS KINGDOM

PRAYER MOMENT

PRAY THAT THE LORD WOULD SEND OUT LABORERS INTO HIS HARVEST (MATTHEW 9:38)

- Pray for **global workers** preparing now for long-term service.

    - Pray that when they experience fear, they would trust in the Good Shepherd who will never leave them nor forsake them.

    - Pray that they would endure the work of preparation with patience, trusting that God will use those efforts and their reliance on him to increase their effectiveness.

- Pray for **future global workers** who, even now, God may be leading to leave their home and cross cultural, linguistic, and physical boundaries to share the gospel and strengthen the church in hard-to-reach places. Pray that their hearts would be soft to the Holy Spirit's leading and that they would respond in obedience and faith.

- Pray for **global workers** who are currently serving in difficult places.

  - Pray that they will trust in God when they labor faithfully but don't see immediate fruit.

  - Pray that God would give them faith to trust that he's working and that their efforts are not in vain, that God's Word never returns void (Isaiah 55:11).

  - Pray that they can establish deep and meaningful relationships with their community, that they would have opportunities to share the gospel fully with the lost around them, and that those people would come to saving faith in Jesus.

GIVE TODAY ♥
MAKE JESUS KNOWN IN INDONESIA, NORTH KOREA, MYANMAR, AND OTHER HARD TO REACH PLACES.

RADICAL.NET/SCGIVE

SUMMARY

THE LIFE THAT COUNTS FOLLOWS JESUS AND MAKES HIM KNOWN IN YOUR NEIGHBORHOOD AND ALL NATIONS.

FOLLOWING JESUS MEANS ENTRUSTING OUR LIVES TO HIS AUTHORITY.

MAKING JESUS KNOWN MEANS SPREADING HIS LOVE WITH HIS AUTHORITY.

AS WE FOLLOW JESUS, WE FIND __rest__ FOR OUR SOULS IN HIM AS OUR KING.

AS WE MAKE HIM KNOWN, WE FIND PURPOSE FOR OUR LIVES AS __Agents__ OF HIS KINGDOM.

MATTHEW 11:1

¹ When Jesus had finished instructing his twelve disciples, he went on from there to teach and preach in their cities.

MATTHEW 11:28-30

²⁸ Come to me, all who labor and are heavy laden, and I will give you rest. ²⁹ Take my yoke upon you, and learn from me, for I am gentle and lowly in heart, and you will find rest for your souls. ³⁰ For my yoke is easy, and my burden is light."

WHEN FAITH IS HARD AND BURDENS ARE HEAVY, JESUS' YOKE IS EASY AND HIS BURDEN IS LIGHT (MATT. 11).

WHEN FAITH IS __Hard__ ...

MATTHEW 11:2-3

² Now when John heard in prison about the deeds of the Christ, he sent word by his disciples ³ and said to him, "Are you the one who is to come, or shall we look for another?"

"Doubt is natural within faith. It comes because of our human weakness and frailty."

"Unbelief is the decision to live your life as if there is no God. It is a deliberate decision to reject Jesus Christ and all that he stands for. But doubt is something quite different. Doubt arises within the context of faith. It is a wistful longing to be sure of the things in which we trust."

— Alister McGrath

*"When the New Testament talks about doubt, whether you're talking about the gospels or the epistles, it primarily focuses on believers. That's very important. It's as if you have to believe

something before you can doubt it; you have to be committed to it before you begin to question it. So doubt is held up as the unique problem of the believer."
— John MacArthur

"Some of us who have preached the Word for years, and have been the means of working faith in others and of establishing them in the knowledge of the fundamental doctrines of the Bible, have nevertheless been the subjects of the most fearful and violent doubts as to the truth of the very gospel we have preached."
— Charles Spurgeon

Difficult Situations

Unmet Expectations

Limited Perception

BOOK OF MATTHEW | SESSION 03

MATTHEW 7:13-14

¹³ "Enter by the narrow gate. For the gate is wide and the way is easy that leads to destruction, and those who enter by it are many. ¹⁴ For the gate is narrow and the way is hard that leads to life, and those who find it are few.

… AND BURDENS ARE ___Heavy___ …

… JESUS' YOKE IS ___Easy___ …

COLOSSIANS 1:27-29

²⁷ To them God chose to make known how great among the Gentiles are the riches of the glory of this mystery, which is Christ in you, the hope of glory. ²⁸ Him we proclaim, warning everyone and teaching everyone with all wisdom, that we may present everyone mature in Christ. ²⁹ For this I toil, struggling with all his energy that he powerfully works within me.

> The yoke is only easy for you when you have Jesus' supernatural __power__ in you.

… AND HIS BURDEN IS __light__.

1 JOHN 5:3

³ For this is the love of God, that we keep his commandments. And his commandments are not burdensome.

> The burden is light for you when you realize how __lovely__ Jesus is and how much he loves you.

WHEN FAITH IS HARD AND BURDENS ARE HEAVY, JESUS' YOKE IS EASY AND HIS BURDEN IS LIGHT (MATT. 11).

SIX PORTRAITS OF JESUS THE KING

JESUS IS THE __Lord__ OF THE SABBATH (MATT. 12:1-14)

MATTHEW 12:8

⁸ For the Son of Man is lord of the Sabbath."

JESUS IS THE __servant__ OF GOD AND SINNERS (MATT. 12:15-21).

MATTHEW 12:19-21

¹⁹ He will not quarrel or cry aloud,
 nor will anyone hear his voice in the
  streets;
²⁰ a bruised reed he will not break,
 and a smoldering wick he will not quench,
until he brings justice to victory;
²¹   and in his name the Gentiles will hope."

JESUS IS THE __power__ OF GOD (MATT. 12:22-37).

Margin note: There is more Mercy in Jesus than there is sin in you!

MATTHEW 12:29

²⁹ Or how can someone enter a strong man's house and plunder his goods, unless he first binds the strong man? Then indeed he may plunder his house.

JESUS IS THE GREATER PROPHET, WISER KING, AND ELDER _Brother_ (MATT. 12:38-50).

MATTHEW 12:41-42

⁴¹ The men of Nineveh will rise up at the judgment with this generation and condemn it, for they repented at the preaching of Jonah, and behold, something greater than Jonah is here. ⁴² The queen of the South will rise up at the judgment with this generation and condemn it, for she came from the ends of the earth to hear the wisdom of Solomon, and behold, something greater than Solomon is here.

MATTHEW 12:49-50

⁴⁹ And stretching out his hand toward his disciples, he said, "Here are my mother and my brothers! ⁵⁰ For whoever does the will of my Father in heaven is my brother and sister and mother."

EIGHT PARABLES OF JESUS' KINGDOM

Listen from the hearer's perspective, look for the ___main___ point, and then let the truth change your perception.

THE PARABLE OF THE ___sower___ (MATT. 13:1-23)

MATTHEW 13:3

³ And he told them many things in parables, saying: "A sower went out to sow.

THE PARABLES OF THE WEEDS AND THE __Net__ (MATT. 13:24-30, 34-43, AND 47-50)

MATTHEW 13:24-25

²⁴ He put another parable before them, saying, "The kingdom of heaven may be compared to a man who sowed good seed in his field, ²⁵ but while his men were sleeping, his enemy came and sowed weeds among the wheat and went away.

MATTHEW 13:47

⁴⁷ "Again, the kingdom of heaven is like a net that was thrown into the sea and gathered fish of every kind.

THE PARABLES OF THE MUSTARD SEED AND __leaven__ (MATT. 13:31-33)

MATTHEW 13:31-32

³¹ He put another parable before them, saying, "The kingdom of heaven is like a grain of mustard seed that a man took and sowed in his field. ³² It is the smallest of all seeds, but when it has grown it is larger than all the garden plants and becomes a tree, so that the birds of the air come and make nests in its branches."

MATTHEW 13:33

³³ He told them another parable. "The kingdom of heaven is like leaven that a woman took and hid in three measures of flour, till it was all leavened."

THE PARABLES OF THE TREASURE AND THE _Pearl_ (MATT. 13:44-46)

MATTHEW 13:45-46

⁴⁵ "Again, the kingdom of heaven is like a merchant in search of fine pearls, ⁴⁶ who, on finding one pearl of great value, went and sold all that he had and bought it.

THE PARABLE OF THE ___Homeowner___
(MATT. 13:51-52)

MATTHEW 13:52

⁵² And he said to them, "Therefore every scribe who has been trained for the kingdom of heaven is like a master of a house, who brings out of his treasure what is new and what is old."

JOHN THE BAPTIST: AGENT OF GOD'S KINGDOM
(MATT. 14:1-12)

FOLLOWERS OF JESUS: AGENTS OF THE KING
(MATT. 14:13-36)

MATTHEW 14:13-21

¹³ Now when Jesus heard this, he withdrew from there in a boat to a desolate place by himself. But when the crowds heard it, they followed him on foot from the towns. ¹⁴ When he went ashore he saw a great crowd, and he had compassion on them and healed their sick. ¹⁵ Now when it was evening, the disciples came to him and said, "This is a desolate place, and the day is now over; send the crowds away to go into the villages and buy food for themselves." ¹⁶ But Jesus said, "They need not go away; you give them something to eat." ¹⁷ They said to him, "We have only five loaves here and two fish." ¹⁸ And he said, "Bring them here to me." ¹⁹ Then he ordered the crowds to sit down on the grass, and taking the five loaves and the two fish, he looked up to heaven and said a blessing. Then

he broke the loaves and gave them to the disciples, and the disciples gave them to the crowds. ²⁰ And they all ate and were satisfied. And they took up twelve baskets full of the broken pieces left over. ²¹ And those who ate were about five thousand men, besides women and children.

JESUS MEETS NEEDS ____IN____ US.

He is the new Moses.

He is the greater prophet.

He is the Messianic host.

JESUS MEETS NEEDS __through__ US.

BOOK OF MATTHEW | SESSION 03

ISAIAH 26:3

³ You keep him in perfect peace

whose mind is stayed on you,

because he trusts in you.

MATTHEW 14:33

1st time disciples proclaim Jesus as Son of God

³³ And those in the boat worshiped him, saying, "Truly you are the Son of God."

Jesus has come to cleanse and satisfy the ___Jewish___ people (Matt. 15:1-20).

Jesus has come to cleanse and satisfy ___all___ peoples (Matt. 15:21-39).

MATTHEW 15:21-28

²¹ And Jesus went away from there and withdrew to the district of Tyre and Sidon.

²² And behold, a Canaanite woman from that region came out and was crying, "Have mercy on me, O Lord, Son of David; my daughter is severely oppressed by a demon." ²³ But he did not answer her a word. And his disciples came and begged him, saying, "Send her away, for she is crying out after us." ²⁴ He answered, "I was sent only to the lost sheep of the house of Israel." ²⁵ But she came and knelt before him, saying, "Lord, help me." ²⁶ And he answered, "It is not right to take the children's bread and throw it to the dogs." ²⁷ She said, "Yes, Lord, yet even the dogs eat the crumbs that fall from their masters' table." ²⁸ Then Jesus answered her, "O woman, great is your faith! Be it done for you as you desire." And her daughter was healed instantly.

The harvest field is __ripe__.

The divine plan is __global__.

MATTHEW 15:29-31

²⁹ Jesus went on from there and walked beside the Sea of Galilee. And he went up on the mountain and sat down there. ³⁰ And great crowds came to him, bringing with them the lame, the blind, the crippled, the mute, and many others, and they put them at his feet, and he healed them, ³¹ so that the crowd wondered, when they saw the mute speaking, the crippled healthy, the lame walking, and the blind seeing. And they glorified the God of Israel.

MATTHEW 15:32-39

³² Then Jesus called his disciples to him and said, "I have compassion on the crowd because they have been with me now three days and have nothing to eat. And I am unwilling to send them away hungry, lest they faint on the way." ³³ And the disciples said to

him, "Where are we to get enough bread in such a desolate place to feed so great a crowd?" 34 And Jesus said to them, "How many loaves do you have?" They said, "Seven, and a few small fish." 35 And directing the crowd to sit down on the ground, 36 he took the seven loaves and the fish, and having given thanks he broke them and gave them to the disciples, and the disciples gave them to the crowds. 37 And they all ate and were satisfied. And they took up seven baskets full of the broken pieces left over. 38 Those who ate were four thousand men, besides women and children. 39 And after sending away the crowds, he got into the boat and went to the region of Magadan.

FOLLOW JESUS AND MAKE HIM KNOWN IN YOUR NEIGHBORHOOD AND IN ALL NATIONS.

FIND REST FOR YOUR SOUL IN JESUS AS YOUR KING.

FIND PURPOSE FOR YOUR LIFE AS AN AGENT OF HIS KINGDOM.

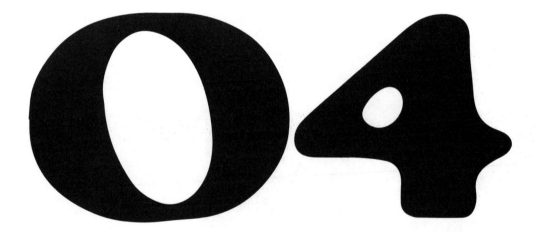

THE CHURCH: THE COMMUNITY OF PEOPLE MAKING THEIR LIVES COUNT

SUMMARY

LIFE IS FOUND IN FOLLOWING JESUS AND MAKING HIM KNOWN IN YOUR NEIGHBORHOOD AND IN ALL NATIONS.

FOLLOWING JESUS MEANS ENTRUSTING OUR LIVES TO HIS AUTHORITY.

MAKING JESUS KNOWN MEANS SPREADING HIS LOVE WITH HIS AUTHORITY.

AS WE FOLLOW JESUS, WE FIND REST FOR OUR SOULS IN JESUS AS OUR KING.

AS WE MAKE HIM KNOWN, WE FIND PURPOSE FOR OUR LIVES AS AGENTS OF HIS KINGDOM.

THE CHURCH: THE COMMUNITY OF BROTHERS AND SISTERS WHO ARE __comitted together__ TO FOLLOWING JESUS AND MAKING HIM KNOWN IN OUR NEIGHBORHOODS AND ALL NATIONS.

MATTHEW 16:13-17

¹³ Now when Jesus came into the district of Caesarea Philippi, he asked his disciples, "Who do people say that the Son of Man is?" ¹⁴ And they said, "Some say John the Baptist, others say Elijah, and others Jeremiah or one of the prophets." ¹⁵ He said to them, "But <u>who do you</u> say that I am?" ¹⁶ Simon Peter replied, <u>"You are the Christ, the Son of the living God."</u> ¹⁷ And Jesus answered him, <u>"Blessed are you, Simon Bar-Jonah! For flesh and blood has not revealed this to you, but my Father who is in heaven.</u>

A TRUE UNDERSTANDING OF CHRIST COMES FROM DIVINE __revelation__, NOT HUMAN INVENTION.

1st mention of the "Church" in the Gospels

MATTHEW 16:18

¹⁸ And I tell you, you are Peter [*means Rock*], and on this rock I will build my church, and the gates of hell shall not prevail against it.

THE CHURCH IS THE COMMUNITY OF PEOPLE WHO FOLLOW JESUS __truly__.

THE CHURCH IS THE COMMUNITY OF PEOPLE WHO MAKE JESUS KNOWN __confidently__.

ACTS 2:36-38

³⁶ "Let all the house of Israel therefore know for certain that God has made him both Lord and Christ, this Jesus whom you crucified." ³⁷ Now when they heard this they were cut to the heart, and said to Peter and the rest of the apostles, "Brothers, what shall we do?" ³⁸ And Peter said to them, "Repent and be baptized every one of you in the name of Jesus Christ

for the forgiveness of your sins, and you will receive the gift of the Holy Spirit.

ACTS 2:41

⁴¹ So those who received his word were baptized, and there were added that day about three thousand souls.

"Nothing can altogether overthrow and destroy [the church]. Its members may be persecuted, oppressed, imprisoned, beaten, beheaded, burned; but the true church is never altogether extinguished; it rises again from its afflictions; it lives on through fire and water. When crushed in one land it springs up in another. The Pharaohs, the Herods, the Neros, have labored in vain to put down this church; they slay their thousands, and then pass away and go to their own place. The true Church outlives them all . . ."

— J. C. Ryle

MATTHEW 16:19

¹⁹ I will give you the keys of the kingdom of heaven, and whatever you bind on earth shall be bound in heaven, and whatever you loose on earth shall be loosed in heaven."

MATTHEW 16:24

²⁴ Then Jesus told his disciples, "If anyone would come after me, let him deny himself and take up his cross and follow me.

Die to yourself.

Follow Jesus.

Find ____life____.

MATTHEW 16:25-27

²⁵ For whoever would save his life will lose it, but whoever loses his life for my sake will find it. ²⁶ For what will it profit a man if he gains the whole world and forfeits his soul? Or what shall a man give in return for his soul? ²⁷ For the Son of Man is going to come with his angels in the glory of his Father, and then he will repay each person according to what he has done.

BEHOLD THE GLORY OF JESUS (MATT. 17:1-13).

BEHOLD THE HUMILITY OF JESUS (MATT. 17:14-27).

THE CHURCH IS COMPRISED OF CITIZENS OF GOD'S KINGDOM AND _children_ OF GOD THE KING.

MATTHEW 18:1-4

¹ At that time the disciples came to Jesus, saying, "Who is the greatest in the kingdom of heaven?" ² And calling to him a child, he put him in the midst of them ³ and said, "Truly, I say to you, unless you turn and become like children, you will never enter the kingdom of heaven. ⁴ Whoever humbles himself like this child is the greatest in the kingdom of heaven.

"What is a Christian? The richest answer I know is that a Christian is one who has God as Father. If you want to know how well a person understands Christianity, find out how much he makes of the thought of being God's child, and having God as his Father. If this is not the thought that prompts and controls his worship and prayers and his whole outlook on life, it means that he does not understand Christianity very well at all."

– J. I. Packer

MATTHEW 18:5-6

⁵ "Whoever receives one such child [christian] in my name receives me, ⁶ but whoever causes one of these little ones who believe in me to sin, it would be better for him to have a great millstone fastened around his neck and to be drowned in the depth of the sea.

We protect one another from sin (Matt. 18:5-9).

We pursue one another in love (Matt. 18:10-14).

We __restore__ one another when we fall into sin (Matt. 18:15-20).

MATTHEW 18:15-17

¹⁵ "If your brother sins against you, go and tell him his fault, between you and him alone. If he listens to you, you have gained your brother. ¹⁶ But if he does not listen, take one or two others along with you, that every charge may be established by the evidence of two or three witnesses. ¹⁷ If he refuses to listen to them, tell it to the church. And if he refuses to listen even to the church, let him be to you as a Gentile and a tax collector.

We __forgive__ one another when we are sinned against (Matt. 18:21-35).

MATTHEW 18:21-22

²¹ Then Peter came up and said to him, "Lord, how often will my brother sin against me, and I forgive him? As many as seven times?"

²² Jesus said to him, "I do not say to you seven times, but seventy-seven times.

A KINGDOM PERSPECTIVE ON __Marriage__
(MATT. 19:1-12)

> Marriage is a gift to be prized and protected.

> Singleness is a gift to be stewarded for the kingdom's sake.

A KINGDOM PERSPECTIVE ON __Money__
(MATT. 19:13-30)

MATTHEW 19:21

²¹ Jesus said to him, "If you would be perfect, go, sell what you possess and give to the poor, and you will have treasure in heaven; and come, follow me."

To follow Jesus is to leave behind short-term treasure we cannot keep for long-term treasure we cannot lose.

To make Jesus known is to show radical generosity to people in need.

A KINGDOM PERSPECTIVE ON merit
(MATT. 20:1-16)

Salvation in the kingdom is all about God's mercy and nothing about our merit.

A KINGDOM PERSPECTIVE ON motive
(MATT. 20:20-28)

Jesus came to serve us.

We live to serve others.

A KINGDOM PERSPECTIVE ON ___mercy___
(MATT. 20:29-34)

We are all desperate for mercy that Jesus alone can give.

MATTHEW 20:33-34

³³ They said to him, "Lord, let our eyes be opened." ³⁴ And Jesus in pity touched their eyes, and immediately they recovered their sight and followed him.

TEN PICTURES OF JESUS

Jesus is the divine King (Matt. 21:3).

Jesus is the prophesied King (Matt. 21:4-5; Zech. 9:9).

Jesus is the gentle King (Matt. 21:4-5; Zech. 9:9).

Jesus is the righteous King (Matt. 21:4-5; Zech. 9:9).

Jesus is the Savior King (Matt. 21:4-5; Zech. 9:9).

Jesus is the peaceful King (Matt. 21:4-5; Zech. 9:10).

ZECHARIAH 9:10b

he shall speak peace to the nations;

Jesus is the global King (Matt. 21:4-5).

ZECHARIAH 9:10c

his rule shall be from sea to sea,

and from the River to the ends of the earth.

Jesus is the Messianic King (Matt. 21:4-5).

Jesus is the holy King (Matt. 21:12-17).

MATTHEW 21:12

¹² And Jesus entered the temple and drove out all who sold and bought in the temple, and he overturned the tables of the money-changers and the seats of those who sold pigeons.

Jesus is the authoritative King (Matt. 21:12-17).

MATTHEW 21:14

¹⁴ And the blind and the lame came to him in the temple, and he healed them.

KINGDOM __confrontation__

(MATT. 21:23-23:39)

On Authority: Confrontation with Temple Leaders (Matt. 21:23-22:14)

The Parable of the Two Sons (Matt. 21:28-32)

The Parable of the Talents (Matt. 21:33-46)

The Parable of the Wedding Feast (Matt. 22:1-14)

On Taxes: Confrontation with Pharisees and Herodians (Matt. 22:15-22)

On the Resurrection: Confrontation with Sadducees (Matt. 22:23-33)

On the Commandments: Confrontation with a Lawyer (Matt. 22:34-40)

MATTHEW 22:37-40

³⁷ And he said to him, "You shall love the Lord your God with all your heart and with all your soul and with all your mind. ³⁸ This is the great and first commandment. ³⁹ And a second is like it: You shall love your neighbor as yourself. ⁴⁰ On these two commandments depend all the Law and the Prophets."

To follow Jesus is to love God supremely.

To make him known is to love others selflessly.

On the Messiah: Confrontation with Pharisees (Matt. 22:41-46)

MATTHEW 22:46

⁴⁶ And no one was able to answer him a word, nor from that day did anyone dare to ask him any more questions.

KINGDOM ___condemnation___
(MATT. 23:1-36)

> Severe Warnings about Dead Religion
> (Matt. 23: 1-12)

> Seven Woes against Religious Leaders
> (Matt. 23:13-36)

KINGDOM ___compassion___
(MATT. 23:37-39)

MATTHEW 23:37

³⁷ "O Jerusalem, Jerusalem, the city that kills the prophets and stones those who are sent to

it! How often would I have gathered your children together as a hen gathers her brood under her wings, and you were not willing!

The church needs leaders who humbly ___submit___ to the authority of Jesus and humbly ___serve___ with the love of Jesus.

The church lives and dies in hopeful anticipation of the ___coming___ of Jesus (Matt. 24-25).

Jerusalem is going to be destroyed.

MATTHEW 24:15-16

15 "So when you see the abomination of desolation spoken of by the prophet Daniel, standing in the holy place (let the reader

understand), ¹⁶ then let those who are in Judea flee to the mountains.

MATTHEW 24:21

²¹ For then there will be great tribulation, such as has not been from the beginning of the world until now, no, and never will be.

Jesus is going to come back.

MATTHEW 24:29-31

²⁹ "Immediately after the tribulation of those days the sun will be darkened, and the moon will not give its light, and the stars will fall from heaven, and the powers of the heavens will be shaken. ³⁰ Then will appear in heaven the sign of the Son of Man, and then all the tribes of the earth will mourn, and they will

see the Son of Man coming on the clouds of heaven with power and great glory. ³¹ And he will send out his angels with a loud trumpet call, and they will gather his elect from the four winds, from one end of heaven to the other.

___Perservero___ in faith: Follow Jesus and make him known until he returns.

You will face deception.

You will face persecution.

You will face temptation.

You will face tribulation.

MATTHEW 24:14

¹⁴ And this gospel of the kingdom will be proclaimed throughout the whole world as a testimony to all nations, and then the end will come.

Stay focused on __mission__!

"God alone knows the definition of terms. I cannot precisely define who all the nations are, but I do not need to know. I know only one thing: Christ has not yet returned; therefore, the task is not yet done. When it is done, Christ will come. Our responsibility is not to insist on defining the terms; our responsibility is to complete the task. So long as Christ does not return, our work is undone. Let us get busy and complete our mission."

– George Ladd

Jesus' delay may feel long.

Jesus' return will be sudden.

His judgment will be irreversible.

Our hearts will be exposed.

Our sentence may be surprising.

Our lives will stand alone.

We must be __prepared__.

BOOK OF MATTHEW | SESSION 04

Two eternal destinations await us all …

1. __Heaven__

MATTHEW 25:34

³⁴ "The King will say to those on his right, 'Come, you who are blessed by my Father, inherit the kingdom prepared for you from the foundation of the world!'"

2. __Hell__

MATTHEW 25:41

⁴¹ "Then he will say to those on his left, 'Depart from me, you cursed, into the eternal fire prepared for the devil and his angels.'"

THE HEIGHT OF HUMAN **sinfulness**

(MATT. 26-27)

Jewish leaders: Rejecting, arresting, accusing, and judging the Son of God.

Roman leaders: Sentencing and crucifying the Son of God.

Soldiers: Stripping, scourging, mocking, beating, and spitting on the Son of God.

Crowds: Ridiculing, reviling, and shouting at the Son of God.

Disciples: Betraying, denying, disobeying, scattering, and deserting the Son of God.

"Until you see the cross as that which is done by you, you will never appreciate that it is done for you."

– John Stott

THE DEPTH OF DIVINE Love (MATT. 26-27)

Substitution: Jesus died our death.

Propitiation: Jesus endured our condemnation (see Ps. 75:8; Isa. 51:17; Jer. 25:15-16).

ROMANS 3:23-25

[23] for all have sinned and fall short of the glory of God, [24] and are justified by his grace as a gift, through the redemption that is in Christ Jesus, [25] whom God put forward as a propitiation by his blood, to be received by faith.

BOOK OF MATTHEW | SESSION 04

MATTHEW 26:39b

"My Father, if it be possible, let this cup pass from me; nevertheless, not as I will, but as you will."

Matthew 26:28 only time "covenant" is mentioned in gospel of Matthew

_____Reconciliation_: Jesus suffered our separation.

MATTHEW 27:45-46

⁴⁵ Now from the sixth hour there was darkness over all the land until the ninth hour. ⁴⁶ And about the ninth hour Jesus cried out with a loud voice, saying, "Eli, Eli, lema sabachthani?" that is, "My God, my God, why have you forsaken me?" Psalm 22

SECRET CHURCH   123

MATTHEW 27:50

⁵⁰ And Jesus cried out again with a loud voice and yielded up his spirit.

MATTHEW 27:65

⁶⁵ Pilate said to them, "You have a guard of soldiers. Go, make it as secure as you can."

MATTHEW 28:1-10

¹ Now after the Sabbath, toward the dawn of the first day of the week, Mary Magdalene and the other Mary went to see the tomb. ² And behold, there was a great earthquake, for an angel of the Lord descended from heaven and came and rolled back the stone and sat on it. ³ His appearance was like lightning, and his clothing white as snow. ⁴ And for fear of him the guards trembled and became like dead men. ⁵ But the angel said to the women, "Do

not be afraid, for I know that you seek Jesus who was crucified. ⁶ He is not here, for he has risen, as he said. Come, see the place where he lay. ⁷ Then go quickly and tell his disciples that he has risen from the dead, and behold, he is going before you to Galilee; there you will see him. See, I have told you." ⁸ So they departed quickly from the tomb with fear and great joy, and ran to tell his disciples. ⁹ And behold, Jesus met them and said, "Greetings!" And they came up and took hold of his feet and worshiped him. ¹⁰ Then Jesus said to them, "Do not be afraid; go and tell my brothers to go to Galilee, and there they will see me."

MATTHEW 28:16-20

¹⁶ Now the eleven disciples went to Galilee, to the mountain to which Jesus had directed them. ¹⁷ And when they saw him they

worshiped him, but some doubted. [18] And Jesus came and said to them, "All authority in heaven and on earth has been given to me. [19] Go therefore and make disciples of all nations, baptizing them in the name of the Father and of the Son and of the Holy Spirit, [20] teaching them to observe all that I have commanded you. And behold, I am with you always, to the end of the age."

MATTHEW 4:19

[19] And he said to them, "Follow me, and I will make you fishers of men."

LIFE IS FOUND IN FOLLOWING JESUS AND MAKING HIM KNOWN IN YOUR NEIGHBORHOOD AND ALL NATIONS.

FOLLOWING JESUS MEANS ENTRUSTING OUR LIVES TO HIS AUTHORITY.

MAKING JESUS KNOWN MEANS SPREADING HIS LOVE WITH HIS AUTHORITY.

AS WE FOLLOW JESUS, WE FIND REST FOR OUR SOULS IN JESUS AS OUR KING.

AS WE MAKE HIM KNOWN, WE FIND PURPOSE FOR OUR LIVES AS AGENTS OF HIS KINGDOM.

THE CHURCH IS THE COMMUNITY OF BROTHERS AND SISTERS WHO ARE COMMITTED TOGETHER TO FOLLOWING JESUS AND MAKING HIM KNOWN IN OUR NEIGHBORHOODS AND ALL NATIONS.

MATTHEW 24:14

¹⁴ And this gospel of the kingdom will be proclaimed throughout the whole world as a testimony to all nations, and then the end will come.

MATTHEW 24:30b-31

they will see the Son of Man coming on the clouds of heaven with power and great glory. ³¹ And he will send out his angels with a loud trumpet call, and they will gather his elect from the four winds, from one end of heaven to the other.

MATTHEW 25:23b

'Well done, good and faithful servant.

PRAYER MOMENT

PRAY THAT GOD MAY OPEN A DOOR TO DECLARE THE MYSTERY OF CHRIST (COLOSSIANS 4:3)

- Pray for opportunities for rising and inexperienced **pastors** to receive biblically sound training and to be rooted firmly in God's Word as they lead churches in the future.

- Pray for **church planters,** especially in places where there is no church, who are boldly sharing the gospel and gathering with believers, possibly for the first time in those places.

  - Pray that God would make a way for them to do this work and to endure long enough to see the church grow in health and to raise up the next generation of leaders.

  - Pray that someday, these churches would send out laborers to plant new churches.

- Pray for **people** throughout the world who are suffering from urgent spiritual and physical needs.

  - Pray for relief from their suffering and for the compassion of Christians to represent the compassion of Christ. If there is a church in their community, pray that these Christians would be equipped to serve the suffering around them.

  - Ultimately, pray that their greatest need, their spiritual need, would be met through saving faith in Jesus Christ.

GIVE TODAY ♥
MAKE JESUS KNOWN IN INDONESIA, NORTH KOREA, MYANMAR, AND OTHER HARD TO REACH PLACES.

RADICAL.NET/SCGIVE

ANSWER KEY

SESSION 1

p. 20-21 - gospel

p. 22-23 - four

p. 24-25 - Savior, Messiah

p. 26-27 - center

p. 28-29 - human, divine

p. 32-33 - present, weak, enemies, Judge

p. 34-35 - Israel, nations, adoration, follows, sin

p. 36-37 - yourself, choose, relationship, follows, known, neighborhood, nations

SESSION 2

p. 50-51 - words, disease

p. 54-55 - disciples, disaster, demons

p. 56-57 - sin, save

p. 58-59 - death, disability, devil

p. 60-61 - work, entrusting

p. 62-63 - spreading, need, danger

p. 64-65 - betrayed

p. 66-67 - Fear, Father, publicly

p. 68-69 - supremely, risk, reward

SESSION 3

p. 76-77 - rest, agents, hard

p. 80-81 - heavy, easy, power, light, lovely

p. 82-83 - Lord, Servant, power, Brother

p. 84-85 - main, sower, net, leaven

p. 86-87 - pearl, homeowner

p. 88-89 - in, through

p. 90-91 - Jewish, all, ripe, global

SESSION 4

p. 98-99 - committed together, revelation

p. 100-101 - truly, confidently

p. 102-103 - life, children

p. 104-105 - restore

p. 106-107 - forgive, marriage, money

p. 108-109 - merit, motive, mercy

p. 112-113 - confrontation

p. 114-115 - condemnation, compassion, submit, serve, coming

p. 116-117 - Persevere

p. 118-119 - mission, prepared

p. 120-121 - Heaven, Hell, sinfulness

p. 122-123 - love, Substitution, Propitiation, Reconciliation

Tonight Your Generosity Can Fuel Gospel Growth in Red Zones

 RADICAL.NET/SCGIVE

bookstore.radical.net

FIND THOUSANDS OF BOOKS AND BIBLES AT DISCOUNT PRICES.

USE CODE MATTHEW25 TO GET 35% OFF ORDERS NOW THROUGH APRIL 30, 2025.

Explore 24 past Secret Church events

ALL AVAILABLE TO STREAM FOR FREE!

THE BOOK OF

SAVE THE DATE!
SIGN-UP FOR UPDATES

DANIEL

SECRET CHURCH 🌐 2026

NOTES

NOTES